KID CHEFS

COOKING WITH DAIRY

Rose Miles

Enslow PUBLISHING

Please visit our website, www.enslow.com. For a free color catalog of all our high-quality books,
call toll free 1-800-398-2504 or fax 1-877-980-4454

Published in 2027 by
Enslow Publishing
2544 Clinton Street
Buffalo, NY 14224

Portions of this work were originally authored by Kristen Rajczak and published as Ingredients for a *Healthy Life: Delicious Dairy Recipes*.
All new material in this edition is authored by Rose Miles.

Cataloging-in-Publication Data
Title: Cooking with dairy / Rose Miles.
Description: Buffalo, NY : Enslow Publishing, 2027. | Series: Kid chefs | Includes glossary and index.
Identifiers: ISBN 9781978548510 (pbk.) | ISBN 9781978548527 (library bound) | ISBN 9781978548534 (ebook)
Subjects: LCSH: Cooking (Dairy products)--Juvenile literature. | Dairy products--Juvenile literature.
Classification: LCC TX759.M674 2027 | DDC 641.67--dc23

Printed in China

Photos Credits: Cover, p. 1 Alexander Prokopenko/Shutterstock.com; cover, p. 1 Peter Hermes Furian/Shutterstock.com; cover, p. 1 ER_09/Shutterstock.com; cover, p. 1 banjongseal324SS/Shutterstock.com; cover, p. 1 Phill Thornton Photo/Shutterstock.com; p. 4, 6, 8, 10, 12, 14, 16, 18 ricorico/Shutterstock.com; p. 5 Pixel-Shot/Shutterstock.com; p. 6 NafiCraft/Shutterstock.com; p. 7 Library of Congress; p. 9 Photoongraphy/Shutterstock.com; p. 9 New Africa/Shutterstock.com; p. 11 Stephanie Frey/Shutterstock.com; p. 12 Dmitry Lityagin/Shutterstock.com; p. 13 Markus Mainka/Shutterstock.com; p. 14 New Africa/Shutterstock.com; p. 15 MariaKovaleva/Shutterstock.com; p. 16 Denis180787/Shutterstock.com; p. 17 Robert Kneschke/Shutterstock.com; p. 19 Foodphototasty/Shutterstock.com; p. 21 Pixel-Shot/Shutterstock.com; p. 23 Igor Normann/Shutterstock.com;

CPSIA compliance information: Batch #QSENS27: For further information, contact Enslow Publishing,
New York, New York, at 1-800-398-2504.

Contents

Recipes in this book may use knives, mixers, and hot stove tops. Ask for an adult's help when using these tools.

Words in the glossary appear in **bold** type the first time they are used in the text.

Cheese, Please!

Say cheese! Did you know that cheese is a dairy product? Dairy is one of the five food groups. Along with cheese, dairy includes all foods made from milk, such as ice cream, butter, and yogurt.

Dairy products are delicious, and they have health benefits too. Read on to find out the great things dairy can do for your body. From the Parmesan cheese on spaghetti to the sour cream on top of a taco, there are so many delicious meals that include dairy. You might just find your new favorite!

Do You Have Allergies?

The **recipes** in this book may use **ingredients** that contain or have come into contact with nuts, gluten, dairy products, and other common causes of **allergies**. If you have any food allergies, please ask a parent or teacher for help when cooking and tasting!

Milk is the basis of all dairy products. Drinking a glass of milk is an easy way to get the health benefits of dairy.

Milk Throughout History

Milk has been part of the human **diet** for more than 10,000 years. People began to use milk as food around the time they began living in communities and raising animals for food.

By the time explorers were heading to the Americas, cow's milk was common in Europe. European dairy cows were brought to North America during the early 1600s. By the late 1800s, milkmen were delivering milk to people's homes in glass bottles. Milk has been a staple in homes ever since.

Tasty Tidbits

While cow's milk is the most popular milk in the United States, other animals' milk is used around the world. This includes milk from goats, buffalo, sheep, and even reindeer!

In Belgium in the 1800s, dogs were trained to deliver milk! They pulled carts carrying milk from farms to local dairies.

What Is Milk?

Milk contains three of the main groups of **nutrients** our body needs: fats, protein, and carbohydrates. You'll see different types of cow's milk at the grocery store. But what's the difference?

Fat is one of the body's major building blocks, but some people don't want to take in too much of it. Dairy companies have found ways to take some fat out of milk.

Whole milk has had no fat removed. In 2 percent milk, about half the fat has been removed. And skim milk has had almost all milk fat removed. People may choose one type of milk over another because of health concerns or how it is used in recipes.

Tasty Tidbits

Your body needs some healthy fats in your diet. Fat can be broken down and used as energy or stored for later use. Dairy is a good source of healthy fats, such as those used to build up your brain and **cells**.

Healthy Chocolate Milkshake

makes 2 big milkshakes or 4 small servings

Ingredients:

2 large, ripe bananas
1 ½ cups skim milk
¼ cup low-fat vanilla yogurt
2 tablespoons cocoa powder
1 teaspoon vanilla extract
ice (about two handfuls, or 8 cubes)

Directions:

1. Cut the bananas into a few smaller pieces. Put into a blender with the cocoa powder, yogurt, vanilla, and milk.
2. Blend together.
3. Add the ice to the blender. Blend until smooth.

Not a fan of bananas? Use strawberries or blueberries instead! However you mix it up, this milkshake will give you a delicious helping of dairy.

Going Through the Process

Today, milk is specially **processed** before people drink it. Fat removal is one part of milk processing. In 1862, Louis Pasteur began heating milk to high temperatures to kill any harmful **bacteria**. By 1895, this practice—called pasteurization—had become standard in dairy companies.

Homogenization is another way milk is processed, especially in the United States. High pressure and heat are used to break up the fat in milk so all parts of it are well mixed. Before homogenization, the fat in milk floated to the top as cream. People would either shake up the bottle of milk to blend it in or skim it off the top.

Ice cream is one of the tastiest dairy products. Ask an adult for help before using the food processor and oven.

Tasty Tidbits

Homogenization is especially important for milk being used to make ice cream! It affects the texture and flavor.

S'more Ice Cream Cake

makes about 9 servings

Ingredients:

Crust:

about 8 ounces of graham crackers
1 cup whole almonds, toasted
3 tablespoons sugar
½ cup (1 stick) light, unsalted butter, melted

Filling:

1 ½ quarts low-fat chocolate ice cream, softened until spreadable
1 cup hot fudge from a jar (not heated)
1 cup marshmallow crème from a jar
2 cups miniature marshmallows

Ingredients:

1. Preheat oven to 350 degrees.
2. Use a food processor or high-powered blender to grind graham crackers, toasted almonds, and sugar. Add melted butter and mix until moist crumbs form.
3. Press crust mixture into the bottom and up the sides of a 9 x 9 pan. Bake about 12 minutes. Allow crust to cool.
4. Spread about half the softened ice cream into the crust. Spoon half of the hot fudge over the top. Freeze until the fudge is set, about 10 minutes.
5. Repeat with the rest of the ice cream and hot fudge. Cover and freeze the cake for several hours.
6. When the cake is frozen, preheat the oven's broiler.
7. Spread marshmallow crème over top of cake. Sprinkle miniature marshmallows in single layer. Broil for about 1 minute, just until marshmallows are deep brown.
8. Serve cake immediately with warmed hot fudge!

Yummy Yogurt

Yogurt has been around for centuries in diets around the world. Today, scientists have discovered lots of health benefits.

Yogurt is cultured. This means it's made by adding certain bacteria to milk and letting the bacteria grow. The flavors of buttermilk, sour cream, and yogurt all come from this **fermentation** process.

Some bacteria are bad, but some are good for you! Cultured dairy products help keep up the populations of good bacteria living in our bodies. Good bacteria help break down food and produce nutrients your body can use for energy.

Tasty Tidbits

Choose your favorite low-fat yogurt and spoon some into a tall glass. Add a layer of nuts or granola and a layer of fruit, such as sliced strawberries. Repeat the layers two more times. Now you have a great yogurt parfait (pahr-FAY)!

Yogurt Veggie Dip

Ingredients:

1 6-ounce container of plain, low-fat yogurt
1 garlic clove, minced
2 tablespoons chopped chives
¼ teaspoon salt
¼ teaspoon pepper
¼ teaspoon dried dill
1 tablespoon lemon juice
vegetable dippers

Directions:

1. Chop garlic clove and chives.
2. Mix all ingredients together. Refrigerate until it's served.
3. Slice the vegetables you want to dip with, such as carrots, bell peppers, cucumbers, broccoli, celery, or cherry tomatoes. Pita chips would taste great too!

This easy recipe gives you all the health benefits of yogurt and a bonus dose of your favorite tasty veggies.

That's Cheesy!

From pizza to sandwiches to pasta and even some desserts, cheese is everywhere! Cheese is another cultured dairy product. It's commonly thought that the first cheese was made in the Middle East. Ancient Greeks and Romans ate cheese, and it was part of the Pilgrims' stores aboard the *Mayflower* as they traveled from England to North America.

There are hundreds of uses for the many tasty types of cheese, such as mozzarella, cheddar, Parmesan, Swiss, brie, feta, and more. Since cheese is a food that's high in **calories**, it should be just a small part of what you eat. Low-fat cheeses are a smart choice for a balanced diet.

Tasty Tidbits

In 2024, more than 14 billion pounds (6.3 million mt) of cheese was produced in the United States alone!

Buttermilk Cheddar Biscuits

Ingredients:

makes 8 to 10 biscuits

2 cups whole-wheat flour
4 teaspoons baking powder
½ teaspoon salt
¼ cup (½ stick) unsalted, light butter, chilled
¾ cup low-fat cheddar cheese, grated
1 cup buttermilk

These biscuits use several dairy ingredients like butter, cheese, and buttermilk. They're made with whole-wheat flour, which is a healthier choice than white flour when baking.

Directions:

1. Preheat oven to 450 degrees.
2. Measure flour, baking powder, and salt into a medium-sized bowl. Mix together with a fork.
3. Cut the ½ stick of cold butter into little pea-sized pieces. Add to the flour mixture. With a fork or your hands, mash the butter pieces into the flour so it looks like crumbs.
4. Stir in the grated cheese.
5. Pour in the buttermilk. Mix together until it's just combined. **Knead** the dough with your hands 8 to 10 times.
6. Sprinkle a little flour on your countertop. Turn the biscuit dough onto the floured surface and press it flat until it's about ¾ inch thick.
7. Use a drinking glass to cut out biscuit rounds, or use cookie cutters to make fun shapes!
8. Put the rounds on an ungreased baking sheet and bake 10 to 12 minutes or until lightly browned.

Vitamins and Minerals

Dairy products are good sources of vitamins and minerals, which are two other kinds of nutrients that make your body work well. The B vitamins found in milk give you healthier skin and blood. The calcium in milk makes your bones stronger. Potassium and magnesium are other important minerals you can get from milk.

Healthy fats help cells grow and repair, and the protein in dairy products also does this in muscles. Drinking a glass of milk can help your muscles repair themselves and grow stronger after playing sports!

Tasty Tidbits

Pasteurization destroys some of the vitamins found in milk. In the United States, some milk and dairy products are fortified with vitamins A and D, which means they've had these vitamins added back into them.

Eating dairy products can be delicious and good for your body.

Saturated Fat

Dairy products are good for you, but as with most foods, too much of them can be a bad thing. Doctors and scientists warn against eating too much saturated fat. It raises the level of cholesterol in your blood. Cholesterol is a waxy substance your body needs to build cells and do other activities. But if too much builds up in the body, cholesterol can lead to many health problems, such as heart disease.

Whole-fat dairy products, such as cheese and ice cream, can contain more saturated fat than you need. It's OK to eat them in small amounts but think of these foods as a special treat—not as something you should eat all the time!

Tasty Tidbits

Some people are lactose intolerant, or unable to break down lactose, which is the main carbohydrate in milk products. Drinking milk or eating ice cream can give them cramps, stomachaches, and worse.

Bite-Sized Cheesecakes

makes 6 cupcake-sized cheesecakes

Ingredients:

Crust:

⅓ cup graham cracker crumbs
1 tablespoon white sugar
1 tablespoon light butter

Filling:

1 8-ounce package low-fat cream cheese, softened
¼ cup white sugar
1 ½ teaspoons lemon juice
¼ teaspoon vanilla extract
1 egg

Add fruit on top before sharing this dessert with family and friends. Blueberries or cherries would make a tasty addition!

Directions:

1. Preheat oven to 325 degrees. Lightly grease a 6-cup muffin pan. You can also use cupcake liners.
2. In a medium bowl, microwave your butter on high for about 15 seconds. Mix in the graham cracker crumbs and sugar. Spoon some of the mixture into the muffin cups until each has about the same amount. Press into the bottom of the cup firmly.
3. Bake the crusts for 5 minutes, then remove them to cool. Keep the oven on.
4. Use a microwave-safe bowl to soften the cream cheese, setting the microwave on high for about 30 seconds.
5. Use a mixer to beat together the softened cream cheese, sugar, lemon juice, and vanilla until fluffy.
6. Mix in the egg.
7. Pour the cream cheese mixture into the muffin cups until each is about ¾ full. Bake for 25 minutes.
8. Allow the mini cheesecakes to cool. Keep them in the refrigerator until you're ready to eat them!

Make Healthy Choices

There are many ways you can include dairy in a healthy diet.

You can replace butter or oil in a recipe with the same amount of low-fat, plain yogurt. This will cut down on fat and add some protein to your baked goods.

Add fruit to yogurt instead of buying the flavored kinds. Try cool combinations like mango and blueberry!

Make your own pizza with a frozen, whole-wheat crust. Add slices of fresh mozzarella and tomatoes for healthy, tasty toppings.

Drink low-fat milk instead of a soda with your meals. A glass of milk is an easy way to give your body lots of the nutrients it needs, while soda provides no **nutritional value** at all.

Why Eat Dairy?

Dairy Makes You Strong

- Dairy contains calcium, phosphorus, and vitamin D, which help your bones grow strong. This includes your teeth too! Protein in dairy helps build and repair muscles.

Dairy Helps with Digestion

- Cultured dairy products benefit the good bacteria in the body. These bacteria help break down food so your body can use the nutrients it needs.

Dairy Gives You Energy

- Carbohydrates in milk are broken down and used for energy. This helps you feel energized and awake to run and play.

Dairy Can Be Hydrating

- Milk is made up of about 87 percent water. Drinking enough water is super important for doing well in sports, thinking clearly, and staying healthy.

Glossary

allergy: a body's sensitivity to usually harmless things in the surroundings, such as dust, pollen, or mold

bacteria: tiny creatures that can only be seen with a microscope. Some can cause illness, while others are helpful.

calorie: a unit of energy in food

cell: the smallest basic part of a living thing

diet: the food one usually eats

fermentation: a process by which an organism changes a sugar or starch into an alcohol or acid in the absence of oxygen

ingredient: a food that is mixed with other foods

knead: to work with dough until it's smooth

nutrient: something a living thing needs to grow and stay alive

nutritional value: the makeup of a food and its impact on the body

process: to move something forward in a set of steps. Also, the set of steps itself.

recipe: an explanation of how to make food

Fact Check

1. Yogurt is __________, which means it's made by adding certain bacteria to milk.
   a. cold
   b. creamy
   c. cultured

2. Healthy fats help_________grow and repair.
   a. cells
   b. energy
   c. water

3. What is NOT a type of cheese?
   a. mozzarella
   b. cheddar
   c. yogurt

Answers: 1. c, 2. a, 3. c

On the Internet

The Dairy Connection: Recipes
www.nationaldairycouncil.org/recipes/Pages/RecipeLanding.aspx
Find creative ways to use dairy in your meals every day.

Dairy Fun Facts
www.southwestdairyfarmers.com/fun_facts
Learn more about where dairy products come from, and search for your next recipe!

Index